The Pet Store

by James Howard
illustrated by Jui Ishida

Harcourt

Orlando   Boston   Dallas   Chicago   San Diego

Visit *The Learning Site!*
www.harcourtschool.com

2 dogs

3 cats

4 birds

5 fish

6 hamsters

7 frogs

The pet store

Requests for permission to make copies of any part of the work should be mailed to the following address: School Permissions, Harcourt, Inc., 6277 Sea Harbor Drive, Orlando, Florida 32887-6777.

HARCOURT and the Harcourt Logo are trademarks of Harcourt, Inc.

Printed in the United States of America

ISBN 0-15-314278-2

7 8 9 10 060 05 04